Myers Barnes'

SECRETS OF
NEW HOME
SALES
NEGOTIATION

How to Achieve "Yes!" Every Time

Myers Barnes

Myers Barnes' Secrets of New Home Sales Negotiation:
How to Achieve "Yes!" Every Time
Myers Barnes

For more information, please contact:
MBA Publications
PO BOX 50 Kitty Hawk, NC 27949
(252) 261-7611
sellmore@myersbarnes.com
www.myersbarnes.com

ISBN-13: 978-0-9820957-1-3

Library of Congress Control Number: Pending

Book Design: Karrie Ross, www.KarrieRoss.com

Disclaimer: This publication is designed to provide accurate and authoritative information in regard to the subject matter covered. It is sold with the understanding that the publisher is not engaged in rendering legal, accounting, or other professional service. If legal advice or other expert assistance is required the services of a competent professional person should be sought.

—From a Declaration of Principles jointly adopted by a Committee of the American Bar Association and Committee of Publishers and Associations.

Dedication

What has outlined my life?
Mom and Dad showed unconditional love.
Scott And Barbara surrounded me with family.
Military school instilled discipline.
Hunter awakened love.
Lorena defines lasting friendship.
Homebuilding gave me a career.
Shirley describes creativity.
Cancer confronted my bravado.
God is my security.

Foreword

Get the Lead Out!

Here they come. Those pesky competitors. And right beside them are your coveted buyers. Tightly clasped in their hands are sharpened pencils, poised and ready to start marking down prices

So, what do you do? You get the lead out. You reach for your own pencil in preparation for scratching through the list price of your models. You convince yourself that it's a strategic move if you want to sell more homes.

Problem is that their pencils are sharper than yours. Buyers can always counter with a lower offer and other builders can continue reducing prices ad nauseum.

Harvard's Michael Porter says, "Cutting prices is insanity if your competition can go as low as you can."

You can't win the price war if that's your only strategy for selling homes. So what <u>should</u> you do?

Get the lead out. It's an expression that originated in William Jenkyn's "Reformations Remora" published in 1646. He wrote, "Shall our reformation have a heel of lead?"

Stop being weighed down by heels of lead and take action. Move it! Justify your home's value instead of defending its price. Walk buyers through the model and demonstrate what makes your homes different from your competition. The fancy name is "differential differentiation;" but it's simply you saying to your buyer, "Look. This is what separates us from whomever you're comparing us to. This is why my homes are a better value."

You see, value isn't about price. It about perception. And that has nothing to do with who has the sharpest pencil.

Table of Contents

Introduction

"Books constitute capital. A library book lasts as long as a house — for hundreds of years. It is not, then, an article of mere consumption, but of capital; and often, in the case of professional men setting out in life, it is their only capital."

—Thomas Jefferson

Here is my personal introduction: New home salesperson or builder, I'd like to introduce you to your new best friend — this book.

It will be your constant companion through the sunshine and the shadows cast by the housing industry. It will speak the truth ... whether you want to hear it or not ... and always be available to offer advice, guidance, support and motivation.

Together, you'll explore new ideas and evaluate tried-and-true ones. It will teach you the secrets about one of the most overlooked and underdeveloped skills in new home sales — negotiation.

You won't find it making demands on your time or whining because it's been left discarded and dusty on some bookshelf. There is one request it makes, however, and that is that you don't judge it by its cover. Spend time getting to know what lies within its pages.

Don't perceive it as merely a "thing," but as a loyal companion that can shorten the long road ahead in the housing industry, lighten the heavy load carried by embattled sales professionals, and salve the weary soul. May it fulfill your dreams as you help others achieve theirs in a new home.

Myers Barnes

CHAPTER 1

Welcome to a New Road to Success

"One's destination is never a place, but a new way of seeing things."

—Henry Miller

It's 6 p.m. on a Saturday. Time to leave the model home where you've been working for the past eight hours. You toss your briefcase and computer into the backseat of your car and slide behind the steering wheel. Slipping the key into the ignition, you give it a gentle turn and the car roars to life. A little foot-pressure applied to the accelerator and, within minutes, the speedometer is registering sixty miles per hour.

Now, you might think that your car is accelerating because you're pushing down on the gas pedal, but that isn't totally accurate. Your car could gain speed even if you never touched the pedal. Take it out of gear on a steep incline and watch it go, or forget to refill the gas tank and you'll be applying some hands-on push-power to get it moving.

So what does make your car go? The simple answer is multiple forces working together. When your car is parked, gravity exerts a downward force and the ground exerts an equal force upward; so your car remains stationary.

Then you climb into the driver's seat, start the engine, put the car into gear, and off you go. Why? Because the engine's force rotates the tires, which push against the ground. This results in the ground "pushing" back. The gripping effort creates traction that persists until it's interrupted or lost. Drive on wet or icy roads, in snow, on loose gravel or in the mud, and your car's wheels will spin trying to recover the traction they need.

A friend had this happen to her when a sudden ice storm stranded her two streets from her home in Maryland. She went over a small hill, lost traction and her car slid into a snow bank. Unfortunately, most of her car was protruding into the roadway. Within seconds, she became a sitting target for the next car that came across the ridge.

Two trucks crested, hit the ice patch, skidded, but regained control. Then a small car being driven too fast came across the hill, lost traction and wham! It slid into my friend's sitting-duck van. More cars followed. By the time a police car arrived to divert traffic, six vehicles were involved. Fortunately, no one was hurt; but those feelings of helplessness, fear and anxiety still plague her.

How does this relate to new home sales?

Many new home salespeople today are experiencing those same fears and feelings of helplessness and anxiety.

We don't know what's on the horizon in the housing industry, but predictions aren't favorable. Even salespeople who were at the top of their game in previous years can't get a grip on today's market. So what do we do? Sit on the sidelines and wait to get hit again? Keep spinning our wheels and going nowhere? Wait it out and hope for the best?

Consider this: If you keep doing what you've been doing and you aren't seeing much, if any, increase in sales, what's missing?

I have the answer: words. That's what is missing. The right words at the right time to close the sale.

I'm not talking chit-chat. I'm not even talking about conversation. I'm talking about using words skillfully to negotiate the signing of a sales contract. That's where the rubber hits the road, isn't it?

You could talk to prospects all week, show them every model home you represent, solicit leads until Doomsday, but if you don't convert them into profitable sales, you're just playing a number's game.

And, unfortunately, for too many builders and salespeople, those numbers are not up.

"How did you learn to negotiate?"

This is the question I'm asked most often as I travel across North America speaking to audiences about new home sales. Before I answer it though, I always ask them a question: "By a show of hands, how many of you have read books, listened to CDs, watched DVDs or attended seminars on the topic of negotiation?"

Of the thousands of people I talk to every year, very few hands are ever raised. These real estate professionals are representing multimillion dollar neighborhoods and they are expected to (1) sell enough homes to support their personal lifestyles, (2) sell them at a price that allows the builder to make a decent profit, and (3) protect the equity of those homeowners who have already purchased.

On a daily basis, they are confronted by new home-buyers who feel entitled to concessions, have shopped the competition, and aren't shy about asking for price cuts. And yet the huge majority of new home salespeople — and Realtors in general — either don't give it much thought or haven't taken the time to learn how to negotiate effectively.

Early in my career, I was one of them. I didn't think much about negotiation. I just wanted to focus on selling as many homes as I could as fast as I could at whatever price I could.

After a year or so of selling, I noticed I was getting the same questions ... the same demands ... the same responses from my buyers month after month. That's when I realized I had to change. Since I had a pretty good idea of what the objections would be, I decided to come up with some ready-made, predetermined responses. That was the beginning of how I learned to negotiate.

I didn't use coercion or a heavy-handed approach that bullied buyers into signing a contract. They wanted to buy a home. That's why they were there with me. So, I listened and responded until we reached a mutually-satisfying agreement.

Was it easy? No. Few things worth achieving seldom are.

Did it make a difference in my sales? A huge difference! Implementing that one change sent my sales over the top, surpassing even my expectations.

Why should you learn to negotiate?

Because, like me back then, your sales probably need a jump-start to get back on track. Just as the forces from the ground and the tires combine to help your car accelerate, negotiating provides the force — the traction — necessary to give you momentum in today's economy.

How does it do that? By following Newton's Third Law: For every action, there is an equal and opposite reaction. For every action your Potential Buyers take... for every obstacle they put in your way ... for every objection they voice ... you are prepared with an opposite and equal reaction because you have become a knowledgeable and skilled negotiator.

"But, Myers, I don't like to negotiate.
It makes me uncomfortable."

I know, but think of it this way. You are a new home sales broker. Get it? A broker. Whether you have that legal title or not, you still broker purchase agreements.

By definition, a broker is someone who "arranges or negotiates a settlement, deal, purchase, contract or plan in exchange for a commission." There are stockbrokers, business brokers, power brokers, pawnbrokers, investment brokers, discount brokers, and broker-dealers. Brokers bring buyers and sellers together to exchange an asset. They complete transactions that are in line with the goals of their clients.

Brokers work with clients to educate them and provide investment options. That is what you do. You broker homes. Sometimes, amid all the negativity and browbeating inflicted upon new home salespeople, it's easy to lose perspective and think of your profession as just a job — even a tough one.

However, the reality is that you have an impact on lives in ways that most professions don't. You broker agreements that affect thousands of people through generations of families. You solve problems. Sell environments where children grow up and parents grow old. You help build communities and work with your buyers to build equity. What you do affects the economy of the nation and the future of its families.

Never doubt how important you are to the health and well-being of America. People don't relocate until you sell. Builders don't build until you sell. Lenders and banking institutions depend upon your sales to fortify their financials.

So, it makes sense that, if this is the profession you've chosen and it's so vital to our country and to your family, you should learn it to the best of your ability. Forget shortcuts and shortcomings. You work with what you have and who you are to achieve greater success in new home sales. One significant way of doing this is by improving your negotiation skills.

Despite a negative perception, negotiating isn't a bad thing. It's an effective way to bridge a gap between what you, your buyers and the builder want. Negotiating is simply taking two ideals and merging them into one deal.

It does take work to evolve into an effective negotiator, but, if you're serious about succeeding in new home sales, it's a skill you absolutely must develop. Not everyone is willing to pay the price, and many won't be disciplined or diligent enough for the long haul; but if you will stay the course, the negotiation skills you learn in this book will enable to succeed where others are failing and will provide the leverage you need to offset a daunting buyer's market.

Why this book? Why now?

Do you know what new home salespeople and builders tell me almost every day? It's this: "Look, Myers, I've got a web site. I'm on Twitter, Facebook and too many social media sites to count. I'm reaching the buyers, but they're all looking for a deal. What can I do? If I don't compromise and offer concessions, they'll buy from my competitors. In case you haven't noticed, it really is a buyer's market today."

I hear what they're saying. I feel their pain. I really do understand the frustration of selling new homes in today's market and having to cope with the three C's: compromise, concessions and competitors. They believe that, if they don't give in to buyer's demands upfront, they will be tossed aside as fast as a dirty shirt.

Basically, it's Economics 101: the Law of Supply and Demand. When the inventory of homes is low and demand is high, we have rising prices and diminishing inventory. The result: a seller's market.

That's where our nation hovered from 2002 until the end of 2006. Homes sold like pancakes at a fundraiser. Buyers lined up to get their fill and lenders were dishing out syrupy-sweet mortgages. Ads screamed the offers: Zero money down! Interest-only loans! No documentation needed! Bad credit - No Problem!

Almost anyone and everyone could qualify to buy a home — even those who knew they couldn't afford it. The Great American Dream was fueled by greed, property-flipping investors and home buyers who bought into the hype and the hope.

While we shouldn't have been surprised when the market "corrected," we certainly seemed to be caught off-guard. What happened? Who can we blame?

How could it switch from a housing boom to a housing bust so quickly?

I have a question of my own: Why does it matter? It is what it is. No amount of wishful thinking or moaning or complaining will change reality. The cold, harsh fact is that the housing market — and America in general — is not going back to the way it was a decade ago. Eventually, the housing market will perform better than it did during its heyday, but definitely not anytime soon. There is no seller's market on the horizon and I have no idea how long we'll be submerged in the depths of a buyer's market.

I'm not clairvoyant. I don't read the stars or teabags and I tossed my crystal ball when it predicted that I'd grow up to be tall, dark and handsome.

I don't claim to have an answer to that question, but I do have a solution to the problem. And that's the reason I wrote this book.

We can't control today's housing market, but we can control our response to it. Another cold, hard fact is that, just because buyers are in the driver's seat today, they don't have to take you for a ride.

With the skills you learn in this book, you will be able to negotiate and navigate your way through any new home sale. As management consultant Peter Drucker pointed out, "The best way to predict the future is to create it."

The bottom line: Stop attending a wake for the housing industry. People are still buying homes. They are buying these homes from someone. It should be you.

CHAPTER 2

20 Secrets of New Home Sales Negotiation

"The real secret of success is
enthusiasm."
—Walter Chrysler

To jump-start the process and push you into a learning curve, I'll share some secrets I've learned through experience. While these will be covered more thoroughly throughout the book, you can refer to this list whenever you need a ready reminder of the negotiation process.

Secret #1:

You are frequently negotiating in some form.

Maybe you're trying to work out a compromise with your relatives regarding family vacations. Perhaps you and some friends plan to meet for lunch and — because of food preferences, time restraints, coupons or pricing — you have to agree on which restaurant would best meet everyone's needs. Or you've had to negotiate with your mechanic, doctor or spouse over expenses. Whether you are actively discussing the terms of a sale or simply rescheduling an appointment, you are negotiating. All I'm proposing in this book is that, since you're doing it anyhow, you should learn to do it more effectively.

Secret #2:

Negotiating will not only help you get what you want, but will also help you give others what they want.

Negotiation is both a sales and a communication tool. When you ask the right questions of a buyer, you learn more about that individual and can better serve the needs of each Potential Buyer. How rewarding is that!

Secret #3:

In all negotiations, both sides want something.

Negotiation can only occur when both parties seek a specific outcome. Otherwise, there would be no reason to start the negotiation process because it would be one-sided. The buyer wants what you have to sell and you want the buyer to have it. You just have to come to terms over the best way to make it happen. So never approach a negotiation feeling you are the only one with a burning desire to make the sale happen.

Secret #4:

Negotiation is used to reach a mutually satisfying goal.

Just like a brochure, web site and model home, negotiation is a tool designed to move Potential Buyers to a decision point and conclude in a win-win home buying experience. Negotiation is not intended be used to manipulate or trick people into making a decision that isn't right for them. It is a process that should be honest and open, encouraging candid and respectful give-and-take conversation.

Secret #5:

When you thoroughly prepare yourself to negotiate effectively, you will avoid a power struggle at the end of the sale.

By the time you reach the conclusion of the sale, usually all the details will be dealt with in an amicable way. So, all that's left is to shake hands, sign on the bottom line and hand over the house keys.

Secret #6:

Don't make assumptions about what buyers want.

Ask questions to determine the Potential Buyer's goals, objectives, expectations, tradeoffs, and to identify possible consequences and solutions. Also understand that buyers often ask for more than they expect to get from you.

Secret #7:

By memorizing preplanned responses, you can listen better to what your buyers are saying.

If you prepare and memorize replies in advance, you won't be mentally trying to form a response while your buyer is talking. You will already know what you are going to say so you can fully focus on what your buyer is telling you.

Secret #8:

Expect most Potential Buyers you meet to object to the price.

Not all of them will, of course, but most of them will show some price resistance. This is natural and predictable. You won't escape it as long as you are selling new homes. So expect it... accept it...maybe even embrace it. Because, when your customers bring up the price, they are interested enough to want you to justify your home's value to them. Jump on this opportunity to give them one benefit after another until they are convinced that the true value of the new home really is reflected in the price — or, better yet, exceeds it!

Secret #9:

You must be your first and best customer.

Before you can successfully sell new homes and neighborhoods to others, you must sell yourself on their value. If you have an issue with the price, you'll transfer that subliminal message to your Potential Buyers. They will pick up on your reluctance, hesitation and lack of confidence. You can't sell what you don't own. You must "possess" the homes you sell and have a sense of ownership in them. Otherwise, you'll find it difficult to sell someone else on a home when you aren't 100 percent convinced of its value. Determine how you feel about the pricing, the construction, the builder, the amenities and the community. If you find yourself lacking, listen to the sales presentation of a colleague or revisit the home's features; not its flaws.

Secret #10:

True commitment equals a check and a contract; not a verbal offer.

Unless you have a check and a contract, you are just having a nice conversation with Potential Buyers — and talk is cheap. If your buyers are hesitant to write you a check to begin the negotiation process, continue asking questions until you can pinpoint why they are reluctant to commit. Identify any objections they have. Respond to their concerns, but don't bend the rule: Prospects must submit a proposal to present to the builder. No exceptions. With no contract, there's nothing concrete to submit.

Secret #11:

The party who concedes home court advantage establishes a pattern for future concessions.

Strive to negotiate within your comfort zone, which is your office, model home or homesite. When you concede this advantage by going to your buyers' comfort zone or to neutral territory, you make the first of what is likely to be many needless concessions. Start strong. Stay strong.

Secret #12:

When fearing a negative response from a buyer, think, "What's the worst that can happen if my compromise terms are rejected?"

We are conditioned to fear failure and intimidation, which can push us to make poor decisions. Instead, consider rejection an opportunity for success. Think like Michael Jordan: In an interview, he explained, "I have missed more than 9,000 shots in my career. I have lost almost 300 games. On 26 occasions, I have been entrusted to take the game winning shot and I missed. I have failed over and over and over again in my life, and that is why I succeed."

You won't sell a home to every buyer you come across, but you will learn from the experience and improve.

Secret #13:

The number one reason negotiation fails is because both parties become emotional and hit an impasse

Emotions can run deep. If your Potential Buyer becomes emotional — angry, upset, demanding, confrontational —

gently employ a counter tactic to bring everyone back into a controlled atmosphere where you can continue a rational discussion. Understand that, with new home buyers, emotional needs and wants are just as important as physical ones.

Secret #14:

Never negotiate in haste.

Successful negotiators realize there are few set-in-stone deadlines. When a buyer counters with a limited-time offer, it's usually a ploy to push you to concede to the lesser offer. Don't be bluffed or pressured into hastily making a move. Say, "If I have to make a decision now, then my answer is no. However, if you can give me a bit more time, my answer may be yes!"

Secret #15:

Master body language.

Study the nuances of body gestures so you know what messages you are sending to the buyer and what the buyer is subliminally telling you. You want your passion and confidence to come across in both your words and your actions. Body language provides tremendous insights when you take the time to "read" facial expressions and body movements. Since visible nonverbal behavior serves as an informal lie detector, you should, whenever possible, avoid negotiating by phone.

Secret #16:

"No" can be the beginning of negotiations.

"No" is a decision waiting to be changed. You can guide the discussion away from the negative response by saying, "Okay. You need to help me here. What exactly are you objecting to? What do you see as the problem?" Or you can say something like, "I'd love to make this new home yours, but the numbers have to work on both sides. How so you think we can make that happen?"

Secret # 17:

Don't take it personally.

It isn't about you, so don't internalize any portion of the negotiation process or worry about what your buyers think of you. Leave personalities and perceptions out of it and concentrate on the purpose and the particulars of the sale. Strip it of emotion and just deal with the naked facts.

Secret #18:

Make sure you're solving the right problem with the right person.

As someone said, "We more frequently fail to face the right problem than we fail to solve the problem we face." To pinpoint the right problem, ask your buyers follow-up questions. Research. Review their goals and yours. Be alert to any disagreements that may be amplified. Confirm that you are dealing with the decision-maker. Seek their help in nailing down the correct problem. Then solve it without having the buyers lose face or confidence.

Secret #19:

Negotiating is working side-by-side to achieve mutually-beneficial goals.

There should be no confrontation in negotiation — just collaboration.

Secret #20:

You don't have to like negotiating to do it.

You just have to understand that this is how the world works. In many countries, negotiations are expected before a purchase is made. So, get with the program. If your sales aren't what they should be, don't bellyache. Negotiate. As the saying goes, "If you stand in your own shadow, then don't complain about the dark."

CHAPTER 3

The Foundation of Negotiation

"There are no foreign lands. It is the
traveler only who is foreign."

—Robert Louis Stevenson

Y ou might think that the process of negotiation began
because of greed or the compulsion to win, but it's actually part of our primal instinct and survival DNA.

Our ancient ancestors would bargain with roots,
berries, animal skins and nature's bounty to get something
they needed and didn't have. Eventually, they gathered in
clans and worked together to protect and provide for their
families. As clans multiplied, commerce mushroomed.

We no longer bargain for survival. Today, we negotiate
to preserve the value of what we have — whether it's
currency or communities.

While it's still a novel concept in America, negotiation
is a common practice in other nations. In India, for

instance, every transaction — from acquiring water chestnuts to wedding dowries — is negotiated. Because price tags are nearly nonexistent there, shoppers go from vendor to vendor negotiating prices for goods and services.

Sabeer Bhatia learned this lesson at an early age. He is an Indian-American entrepreneur who cofounded the Web-based email system Hotmail (the name came from HTML, the programming language of Web pages). He says the negotiating skills he learned in his homeland's vegetable markets helped him keep his cool when, at age 28, Bill Gates approached him about buying his company.

Bhatia met with Gates and then was escorted into a large conference room where 12 Microsoft negotiators awaited. They made him a take-it-or-leave-it offer of $160 million for Hotmail. Although he admits to feeling intimidated, Bhatia remained unruffled. He told the negotiators, "I'll get back to you."

As he explained later, he didn't know how to sell a company, but he did know how to buy onions. So, when the negotiations began, Bhatia was on familiar ground. He countered Microsoft's offer with $700 million. They told him that was ridiculous and he was out of his mind.

Bhatia stood his ground amid walkouts, swearing and insults and, within 30 days and on his 29th birthday, Microsoft paid him and his investors $400 million for their little startup. This was in 1997. Today, Hotmail is valued around $6 billion.

As evidenced by the exchange between Microsoft negotiators and Bhatia, veteran hagglers know that the first offer is always the lowest offer. Keep that in mind when Potential Buyers throw out a low-ball price on a home. They are aware that their initial offer probably won't be accepted, but what do they have to lose? They are on a fishing expedition and you might bite.

Experienced negotiators also know that they have the most bargaining power just before close of escrow, so be prepared for buyers to ask for one more thing as they prepare to sign the contract. This is especially true if you've held the price point on the home. They want a final concession to validate their negotiation skills.

Savvy homebuilders will anticipate this and have something set aside that can be thrown in to sweeten the sale and seal the contract. This can be upgrades on the appliances or lighting fixtures, a year of lawn care, the services of an interior designer, a voucher for a moving company, an irrigation system for the yard or gift cards to home-improvement stores.

Everyone isn't from Kansas.

Because today's housing market is multicultural, you need to grasp the principle that people born in other countries aren't being rude or pushy when they barter, bicker, haggle, negotiate or whatever you want to call it. This is the foundation on which their lives and business dealings have been built.

Admittedly, it can be a problem when they try to renegotiate a housing contract they've already signed.

Their intentions aren't to be unethical or unreasonable. They may be from what's called a "high-context" communication culture.

In their country, their culture provides the framework for all communication. They speak less, but infer more, expecting you to derive the information you need from their culture ... observing their way of life, customs, heritage and society.

In contrast, America is a low-context communication country. We expect to have everything in writing. We want contracts; not context.

People from high-context countries — France, Russia, Italy, Spain, China, Japan, India, etc. — view a contract as something that can be changed as relationships deepen and the parties get to know one another better. Along with this, they believe that all parties involved in the agreement are obligated to help one another fine-tune the contract until it meets everyone's needs. That's not a bad thing.

If you develop the mindset that everyone you meet welcomes the opportunity to negotiate, it will help you overcome your reluctance when they begin to bargain.

Here are a few additional points to keep in mind:

1. Never allude that there may be room to negotiate.

When you are working for a builder or developers, by law you are representing their best interests. Your actions should be centered on delivering the most positive outcome for your seller, which is (and this should go without saying) a profitable sale ... not just a sale. You are not the buyer's agent, so don't take on the role of one. The moment you negotiate for the buyer, you switch from seller's representative to buyer's buddy — and that puts you on the weaker side of the negotiation. You present offers from the buyer, but you don't negotiate terms with the builder and try to persuade him or her to accept them. It's a fine line that's easily crossed. Just remember, you negotiate for the builder/developer...not with the builder/developer.

2. Negotiation is a mindset.

Successful negotiators know that they must be fully invested in this strategic endeavor. Just like an actor, you have to buy into the character you're portraying and believe in what you're saying. That doesn't mean you become phony and spew false claims. Just as you wear different hats in life (spouse, mother, parent, club president, father, son, choir singer, bowler, child, volunteer, etc.), you take on a new role when you're representing a builder or developer. For that period of time, you are a professional new home salesperson.

To play the part well, you must be confident in what you are saying and in what you are selling. If you believe in the value of the new homes and community you are offering, you will stay strong and focused on profitability.

Tapping into a negotiator's mindset allows you to work through the sales process with power and control.

Then you succeed in:

- Eliminating objections voiced by the buyers.
- Increasing their level of interest.
- Reducing their anxiety.
- Establishing a value curve that's relative to your competition and to your buyers' needs.

3. Acknowledge and accept that both sides want something.

You want your Potential Buyers to become owners and they want to own a home or homesite. There's your common ground. So never approach the negotiation table feeling as though you are the only one in need. Both parties desire the same outcome or there would be no reason to conduct a negotiation. Remind yourself of this if you begin to question your position.

The person with the most information is usually the one who comes out on top in negotiations.

Learn as much as you can by asking questions and drawing your prospects into the dialogue. Seek to identify underlying problems instead of taking what they say at face value. Research their culture ahead of time so you know what to expect and how to respond.

CHAPTER 4

Preparing to Negotiate

"If I had eight hours to chop down
a tree, I'd spend six sharpening
my axe."

—Abraham Lincoln

The U. S. Navy Seals have a motto: The more you sweat in training, the less you bleed in battle.

The Old Testament recounts the story of Jeremiah, a boy destined to be a prophet. God instructed him to use the days of peace to fortify his mind so he'll be ready when the wars start. Jeremiah 12:5: "If you have raced with people on foot and they have worn you out, how can you compete with horses? If you stumble and fall down in a land of peace, how will you manage in the thick thorn-bushes along the Jordan?"

Muhammad Ali put it this way: "I run on the road long before I dance under the lights."

Louis Pasteur observed, "Chance favors the prepared mind."

And, if you will allow me one more, Colin Powell nailed it. "There are no secrets to success. It is the result of preparation, hard work and learning from failure."

You've probably conquered the "working hard" and "learning from your mistakes" portions. How are you doing on preparation?

Whether it's the military, the warfront, sports, science or selling, preparation is a key component of success; and, in new homes sales, negotiation is a key component of preparation. All the work is performed ahead of time, not during the actual negotiation process. Consequently, the person who is best prepared achieves the most favorable outcome and keeps the discussion on track.

Before negotiations even start:

1. Be absolutely clear in your own thinking about what you expect from the negotiation process. What is the outcome you want? What has been the outcome in the past? What precedents have been set? Have past concessions had an impact on property values?

2. Determine the concessions you are willing to make. What are you comfortable offering in order to reach a "yes" agreement? All concessions, price modifications or incentives should be decided in advance.

3. Review your options. Understand the difference between a discount and an incentive. A discount is, in reality, a price apology. It's basically saying, "Hey, for

whatever reasons, we seem to have priced the home too high and now we need to reduce the price to its true value." Unfortunately, each time you discount a home, you influence property values because they are rooted in comparable sales.

On the flip side, an incentive is added value. Incentives may include upgrades (such as granite counter tops), paid closing costs, no loan-origination fees, or any number of "carrots" that sweeten the deal without souring property values. Incentives should be time sensitive and tailored to create urgency. You would say to the buyer, "If you purchase your new home by (date), we can include these options/features/amenities at no additional price." Another advantage of offering incentives over discounts is that they increase the home's value instead of reducing it.

When using incentives, keep this in mind:

- An incentive is a closing tool and not to be used up front as your opening statement. Far too many times the builder gives the salesperson the tool of an incentive and it is immediately misappropriated because the salesperson uses it at the beginning of the sale. He says something like, "Welcome to Vista Estates. As you look at our homes today, please keep in mind that if you see something you like, we have $20,000 in upgrades and will pick up all your closing costs and origination fees." The Potential Buyer thinks, "Hmm, if he gives me all this and I haven't asked for anything, I wonder what he'll give me if I act reluctant. How far can I push this person?"

- Ignore the discomfort you might feel initially and resist the urge to blurt out the incentives when your customer asks, "What kinds of deals or incentives are you giving today? The other builder is offering _____."

- Do not share the incentive before the buyer asks for one. It's easy for salespeople to think that everybody else is throwing incentives at the feet of buyers, so how can they compete with that? Their conclusion: Throw out incentives immediately to "hook" the prospect. This can backfire, however, because home buyers may think, "What's wrong with this home that they have to bribe me buy it?"

- In reality, when you offer an incentive up front, it isn't a hook or a bribe. It's a discount that translates into a price apology to the buyer. It's like saying, "Hey, you know what? We priced this home at $500,000 hoping you'd spend that much for it, but now we see that you aren't, so we're throwing in $50,000 in upgrades to bring the price down to what it should have been anyhow." Instead of doing this, sell the home, its features, the community, the builder and the amenities. Spotlight the home's value. Cultivate the buyers' appetite for owning it. If you sell the home right, they'll want to buy it; and if they want to buy it, they will want to negotiate the price. That's a given and that is when you throw in the incentives — to please and appease your buyers. You explain, "I am so glad you're interested in purchasing this home. Now, let me tell you we are able to offer that increases its value even more."

- If you discuss incentives before showing the home, there is no basis of value – you are sharing incentives based on nothing, "I'll give you 50% off something." Exactly what? There is no basis of value that has been established. You are selling the deal before selling the house...it's akin to spilling your popcorn in the lobby before the movie starts. Instead, follow this script:

Potential Buyer: "What kinds of deals or incentives are you offering?"

You: "I'm glad you asked! We offer impressive homes, a wonderful location, an incredible school district, fantastic customer service and we are an Energy Star™builder.

As you can see, we have a lot to offer! Not only that, when you find a particular home you want to own, we have some tremendous financing incentives as well."

You: (emphasizing incentives and one-of-a-kind homesites) "We offer no incentives that apply across the board. Instead, our incentives differ from home to home. They can be a substantial amount, yet they will vary based on the particular home/homesite you choose and the timeframe you need for moving. The first step is to select a home you really like and then we can discuss the incentive as it applies to that one-of-a-kind home."

4. Know your buyers and the subject matter. Remain focused so you can separate Potential Buyers from the concessions they present. What do they want and why do they want it? What are their needs as opposed to their wants? Do you sense this discussion will turn it into a power struggle? If so, how will you handle it and still maintain control?

5. Rehearse. Think through the process and the problems in advance. Consider the obstacles and be prepared to respond with a reasonable solution. Practice negotiating with a colleague. To boost your confidence, negotiate during routine activities, such as when you're shopping in retail stores, hiring someone to cut your grass, getting your car repaired, or dining out. In many instances, you can simply ask, "What kind of discount are you offering today?"

6. Maintain your power to walk away. This is especially challenging in today's housing market when sales are slow, but it's better to walk away from a sale than to give too many concessions. That sets a bad precedent. Besides, contrary to what salespeople seem to believe, lowering the price or throwing in incentives does not solve all problems; so why start there?

CHAPTER 5

Planning to Negotiate

"Seek first to understand, then
to be understood."

—Steven Covey

Whats the difference between planning to negotiate and preparing to negotiate? Here's a hint: It's the same difference as between planning a trip and preparing for the trip.

Preparation requires hands-on work. Planning involves forethought and a to-do list.

When you plan a trip, you sit down with a map and travel brochures and write out an itinerary. You set your budget, make reservations and gather information about where you want to go.

When you prepare for your trip, you pack your bags, gas up the car, work for a year to accrue vacation time, save your money and stop delivery of your newspaper and mail.

When you plan to negotiate on the sale of a new home, you map out your strategy, organize your thoughts, research your competition and schedule appointments. Once the planning is done, then you prepare to negotiate. You practice what you will say, talk with the builder about options and incentives, meet with Potential Buyers, have your paperwork handy, stage the model home, etc.

To do one without the other would be like planning a large family cookout and not preparing any food. Or having a huge feast spread out on the table and neglecting to invite anyone to attend.

While you may feel you are experienced enough to quickly dive into preparing without planning, you're wrong. A lawyer is, in effect, a negotiator who is trying to negotiate the best outcome for his client. Imagine a lawyer going into court without having listed and interviewed all the potential witnesses or carefully reviewing all police reports and noting potential problem areas. Is this the advocate you would want? Do you think your builder or buyer wants a salesperson who hasn't planned the negotiation process?

Here are five key planning steps:

1. Thoroughly study the negotiation process and tactics. By the time you finish reading this book, you should have the preparation, planning, phases and problems of negotiation nailed down. Naturally, that doesn't mean you shouldn't read and study more on the topic.

2. Organize, reorganize and understand with absolute clarity what you are seeking to accomplish. Determine your goals for each negotiation. Are you striving to obtain the sale at a specific price point? Do you know what concessions you can and cannot make? Take the time to develop a crystal-clear vision of where you want to end up before the negotiations wind down.

3. Have a written plan of action. Every negotiation is important, so you should take the time to put your thoughts, ideas, tasks and goals on paper. When you write it all out, your thinking becomes focused. As you see the plan take shape, you may notice gaps that should be addressed or see opportunities in which you can reinforce your negotiating position. By not planning and preparing, you could miss a key piece of information and ignore a small step that could make a big difference in the outcome.

4. Think through the entire negotiation process in advance. Just as you think through the places you'll visit on vacation, the roads you'll take and the rest stops and restaurants you'll hit, think through all the stop-and-go portions of negotiation. Indulge in some mental role-playing. What kinds of personality types are your buyers? What is their agenda? What is yours? Move from your side of the table to their side and map out how they will respond and react. It will give you a pretty good idea of which direction your negotiation process will take.

5. Plan your responses. Don't ad lib or shoot from the hip. Have stock comments ready. If you memorize the tactics and counter tactics outlined in this book, you will remain one step ahead of your Potential Buyers.

6. Don't ever bluff. Have a plan. Stick to it. Be prepared to let the prospects walk away and never promise something you can't deliver.

7. Be concise and move quickly. Ambiguity has no place in negotiating.

CHAPTER 6

The Myth of Price Resistance

"Use discretion when negotiating,
which simply means raising your
eyebrow instead of your voice."

—Myers Barnes

Let's debunk the greatest misconception in new home sales: The buyer is only concerned with getting the lowest price.

Many salespeople and builders/developers think this is true, but it's really a myth and I can prove it. If buyers were only focused on price, all you'd have to do is sharpen your pencil and drop prices until your homes sell.

Truth is, buyers are concerned with more than price. They want value — which is what they consider to be a fair price for the features and quality of the home.

Oh, sure, they ask questions such as, "What's the best you can do on price?" or "Will you take less than the listed price?" or "How much does this house cost per square foot?" The last question is especially frustrating when you haven't even had a chance to fully present your neighborhood and new homes. Equally disheartening is hearing them say, "We can't go over a certain amount," or the classic, "Your competition is cheaper!"

The harsh reality is that you'll never escape price resistance as long as you are selling new homes. So you should just accept it. No ... even better ... embrace it! Know why? Because when your customers mention price, they are indirectly asking you to justify your home's value to them. They are interested enough to want to know more. That's a good sign.

Seize this opportunity to actually sell them on the many benefits of buying one of your homes. This action alone will separate the order takers from the professional new home salespeople. You must show Potential Buyers one benefit after another until they are convinced that the true value of the new home is reflected in the price — or, better yet, exceeds it!

The Basic Points of Price Resistance

Point #1:
It always costs too much.

Almost every Potential Buyer will ask the price of a new home and then, when told, flinch. Buyers are intoxicated with the idea of obtaining a "bargain," especially today when popular web sites like Groupon and LivingSocial drop daily bargains into subscribers' emails. This goes back to our basic instinct of wanting something for nothing. We feel good when we know we've received the best price possible. However, the paradox is that, regardless of what price you quote, the customer's initial reaction is likely to be, "Unfortunately, that's really more than we want to pay." I'm sure it is, but that doesn't mean the price isn't justified and that you can't wake them up to that fact.

Point #2:
Price is the common denominator.

Why does price come up so early in the sales presentation? Because it represents something we all have in common: the concern for money — or, more accurately, the concern for saving money. We all relate to dollars and cents. We want to keep as much as possible and spend as little as possible.

Now, here's the real question: Are your Potential Buyers objecting to the price — or are you? How do you feel about the pricing of your new homes in relation to the value of the neighborhood and the property?

Be honest. If you have an issue with it, you'll convey that subliminal message to your customers. They will pick up on your reluctance...your hesitation...your demeanor. How can you even begin to overcome their objections when you feel the same way? In the real world, you can't effectively sell a home if you aren't 100 percent convinced of its value.

If you do find you aren't totally satisfied that the new homes you sell represent a great value to the buyer, then do one of three things: (1) Revisit the property's amenities and benefits. (2) Listen to the sales presentation of a respected and successful colleague. (3) Pinpoint why you aren't totally sold and talk to your builder or sales manager about it.

Remember, professional selling is a process of transferring your emotions and beliefs to the home buyer. In order to be believable, you must believe. If you want to be convincing, you must be convinced. Believe in your neighborhood, housing designs and pricing to fully link your emotions to those of the buyer.

Some salespeople offer bargain-chip incentives, reducing the price and going to almost any extreme to get a sale. Any low-level order taker can give away his or her homes, upgrades and services at a cheaper price.

That's a painless way to make a sale — but not a profitable one. Professional new home salespeople understand the true value of their homes and convincingly convey that to their buyers.

Don't lower your standards or your prices just to get a sale, especially when it slices through your builder's profitability and diminishes the brand value of the company. Remember, bona fide selling communicates value. Reducing the price communicates a lack of value.

Don't Confuse Goal With Bottom Line.

A Ruby-throated Hummingbird must consume twice its body weight in food each day. This is not a goal. It's the bottom line. Otherwise, it couldn't live.

To survive in new home sales, don't confuse your goal with the bottom line. Your goal is what you want to achieve. Your bottom line is what you need to achieve.

Your goal is to sell new homes. Your bottom line is to sell them at a price that results in a profit for you and your builder. If you are just moving product, but not making any profit, why do it?

Many salespeople start compromising in their heads before negotiations even start. This is comparable to having a small leak that sinks a big ship. With this kind of mindset, their negotiating power is ebbing away and eroding profitability. The eventual result is what we've seen happen nationwide — builders are going under because of anemic balance sheets.

Take a tip from the hummingbird and keep your focal point where it belongs — on the bottom line and not on selling homes at any cost.

To do this, help buyers understand that any discount they are requesting is not against the purchase price, but off the net profit.

Explain it to them this way:

YOU: "I know, Mr. & Mrs. Homebuyer, that $5,000 does not seem to be a large amount to ask the builder to discount on this $200,000 home. On the surface, it seems like you're just asking for a 2.5 percent reduction. However, in reality, the discount you are asking for is not off the sales price, but off the profit."

"Here's how it works. Our builder operates on a pre-taxed, gross profit margin of about 10 percent or $20,000. When you ask for a $5,000 discount, it would be taken out of the $20,000. So, instead of a 2.5 percent reduction, you're requesting a 25 percent reduction. That's quite a lot."

"That request also hits a little closer to home with you. Since real estate values are determined by comparable sales, the fastest way to cause a drop in property values for home buyers like you and for communities is to negotiate a lower price."

"You've probably seen or heard on the news what's happened to home values across the nation in neighborhoods that have a lot of short-sales or foreclosures.

A professional appraiser determines a property's market value based upon recent sales of comparable properties in that area. When properties are sold for reduced prices — regardless of whether it's the result of a short-sale, foreclosure or discount — all property values are affected."

"If someone purchased a home yesterday for $350,000 and today another person purchases the same model for $300,000, and tomorrow someone negotiates the builder down to $275,000, then what is the true value of that home? The answer is obvious: $275,000. This translates into a $75,000 equity meltdown on homes in that community."

"Mr. and Mrs. Homebuyer, we do everything we can to protect the value of homes within our neighborhood and, consequently, the equity in your home. If a brand new home is going to be one of your single largest investments, then isn't it reassuring to know that you are doing business with a builder who is concerned with guarding your personal equity and protecting the assessed value of the community?"

At this point, you stop talking and allow the logic to sink into the minds of the buyers.

It is absolutely essential that you and all new home salespeople grasp the importance of holding the price for the sake of the builder and the buyer.

CHAPTER 7

The Four Phases of Negotiation

"The art of discovery consists of
seeing what everybody has seen and
thinking what nobody has thought."

—Nobel Prize winner Albert von Szent-Gyorgyi

Negotiation is a process of discovery. It requires communication — both verbal and nonverbal. Through asking and answering questions, you discover what your buyers want and need in a home.

Just like a chess or tennis match, there is action and reaction. If you're prepared, you will be able to anticipate the next move and position yourself properly instead of impulsively reacting to it.

Here are four phases you'll navigate while guiding your buyer toward a decision.

PHASE ONE:

Confirm.

Before you begin to negotiate, establish one core truth: Does your prospect sincerely want to own a new home or homesite?

Everything else in your presentation and in the negotiation process revolves around this one confirmation. Establishing this levels the playing field. You know where you stand and that you aren't just dealing with a "tire kicker." Your Potential Buyer is comfortable having everything out in the open.

As the relationship progresses, you will be able to determine his or her level of commitment.

PHASE TWO:

Explore.

This phase can be time-consuming because you are exploring the great-unknown regions of your Potential Buyer's psyche. Your purpose is to (1) identify the reasons you are at a stalemate and aren't making progress; (2) discover why your buyer isn't moving forward; (3) lock into any problems that need solutions; and (4) analyze the situation so you can build a framework for your proposal.

Don't rush through this phase. Take the time to gather the facts you need to make an educated move.

Before continuing to Phase Three, you need a check and a contract. If you don't have them, you are merely engaging in idle talk. If your Potential Buyers are hesitant to write you a check to begin the negotiation process, continue exploring until you can pinpoint where their minds are and why they are reluctant to commit. The more knowledge you have about the situation, the better equipped you are to steer toward a successful result.

PHASE THREE:

Propose.

In most real estate transactions, Potential Buyers have expectations. They expect to negotiate based on the accepted practice. This tradition may be reflected in your propositions and/or how you present the contracts.

If your contracts include the words, "Offer to Purchase," change them. Also avoid using these phrases:

> "Let's make an offer!"
>
> "You will never know unless we ask."
>
> "By law I'm obligated to present any and all offers."
>
> "This home is listed at $__ ."
>
> "The price they are asking is $___ ."

Don't allow yourself to conform to the expectations of a Potential Buyer. Be dynamic and innovative. When your Potential Buyers cannot fit your approach into a preconceived notion of a "sales pitch," you have greater control over the negotiations.

PHASE FOUR:

Agree.

The goal of negotiation is to forge a contract that is beneficial and agreeable to all parties. You achieve this by working through the written proposal, one section at a time. Along the way, you will answer the buyers' questions, allay their fears and reaffirm that you truly do have their best interests in mind when helping them find the home they want.

When you first sit down together to hammer out the details, say something upbeat, such as, "Well, I'm excited about nailing down these final details so you can walk out of here with the home of your dreams! Are you ready?" Discuss each point, get the Potential Buyer's approval and move on. If you find yourself stuck on one point, suggest that you return to it later. Keep the pace steady and the tone positive.

You will find, when you've gone through enough negotiations that the successful process will flow like this:

Rehearse. Study what you will say and practice saying it before you ever meet your buyers.

Report. Tell the buyers what the offer is and sell them on the value of the home.

Reconsider. If the buyers counteroffer, review what they are requesting.

Request feedback. Talk to the buyers. Ask questions to distinguish what they want, need and prefer.

Identify where the weak areas are in your presentation and in their perceptions. Listen to them. Follow your written agenda and try to get a handle on their hidden agenda.

Respond. Counteroffer with incentives and concessions that close the gap.

Resolve. Complete the contract.

CHAPTER 8

Danger! Danger!

"Always get to know the other party.
Never negotiate with a stranger."

—Somers White

A rip current is a real danger where I live near the Atlantic Ocean. This strong channel of water rapidly flows sideways near the shoreline, tucked within the churning waves. Anyone caught in its current can be pulled out to sea at speeds of up to eight feet per second. Once trapped, swimmers tend to fight against it, which often leads to exhaustion and drowning.

Rip currents cause the deaths of more than 100 people each year on America's beaches and account for 80 percent of the rescues that beach-front lifeguards perform. They are strongest when the surf is rough. Lifeguards patrolling the beach in my town are on high alert for sudden changes in the surf and will insert poles with red flags in the sand to warn swimmers of an increased hazard from rip currents.

The process of negotiating mimics the movement of the ocean's current. Negotiations can flow smoothly until suddenly there's a change. You hit a rough spot. The tide turns. A buyer gets agitated...disturbed...stirred up over something.

Swimmers caught in a rip current are told to stay calm, not to fight it and to swim with the current until they reach calmer waters. The same advice applies in negotiations. Don't lose your cool. Patiently go with the flow until your buyers calm down.

Potential Buyers will voice their opinions, ask for concessions and assert their objections throughout the sales process. Instead of fighting them to the point of exhaustion, immerse yourself in the negotiation process. To help you sail — and sell — through, here are some red flags to watch for that will warn you of potential rip-current situations.

Red Flag #1:
Assumptions.

We can be quick to assume that our buyers want what we want. So, we conduct negotiations in the same way we would if we were in their position. Bad idea.

Personalities, perceptions and presumptions influence negotiations. To remain buoyant throughout the negotiation process, you need to slice through them and target the real issues.

Identify your buyers' interests, emotions, positions, goals and concerns. Wrap your head around their perspectives before explaining your own point of view.

Red Flag #2:
Lack of knowledge

Know yourself — strengths, weaknesses, flaws and virtues — better than others do. Then study your buyers' mannerisms. Listen to their words. Watch their body language. Tune into their thoughts and emotions. Know them nearly as well as you do yourself. Don't center discussions on numbers until you have this knowledge.

Red Flag #3:
Losing home court advantage

Whenever possible, negotiate on your home turf or in a neutral area. When you are in someone else's territory, you take yourself out of your comfort zone and this can psychologically weaken you. Plan meetings in your office, model home, or at another place where you feel comfortable and in control.

Red Flag #4:
Fear of titles

From a young age, we are taught to obey parents, teachers and authority figures. Titles such as "Doctor" or "Professor" conjure up those feelings of insecurity and inadequacy. To neutralize this fear, get away from the title. When introduced to Dr. William Smith, or John Jones, Vice President, simply say: "Mr. Jones, my name is _____. Is it okay if I call you John?" Or you could say, "Dr. Smith, I'm Sam Superachiever. Please call me Sam. Would you prefer that I call you William or Bill?"

Red Flag #5:
Intimidation

It happens. Here you are, talking amicably with a Potential Buyer, when she casually mentions that she needs to find a zero-gravity chaise for the deck of their yacht docked at the marina. Or he comments on the summer-long trip they took to Italy and the condo they have on the oceanfront. Or someone with celebrity status and draped in diamonds is demanding your attention.

I know. It's enough to make you ... well, never mind. The point is that, when negotiating with those perceived to have social or financial advantages, you may feel a bit intimidated and, subsequently and subconsciously, relinquish power to them.

Don't be sucked into the game of one-upmanship or perceive them to be on a higher level than you. Accept them as equals. They are ordinary folks who may have a few more high-end possessions than you at the moment. However, there is one thing you do have that they don't. That, of course, is the new home they are interested in buying. So ... who is really the person with the power?

Red Flag #6:
Charisma.

He oozes charm. She is so charismatic you want to bask in the warmth of her smile. People who are poised, positive and pleasant can easily sway us. Somehow, even without us noticing it, they are able to effortlessly establish an emotional connection with us. Combine their charisma with a title, and we can be overwhelmed. When you find yourself in this situation, remember that falling victim to their charms will have consequences. Your focal point should be the deal; not their appeal.

Red Flag #7:
Fear of rejection

Unfortunately, we are conditioned to fear failure and rejection, which can push us to make some poor decisions. If you dread getting a negative response from a buyer, think, "What's the worst thing that could happen?"

Answer: They reject the offer. Not you. Consider rejection an opportunity to improve. Learn from it, but don't fear it.

Red Flag #8:
Fear of confrontation.

Disagreement is inherent in negotiations. Piggy-backed on disagreement is usually some form of conflict. While being a peacekeeper is commendable, there are salespeople who take it to the extreme. They are determined to avoid conflict at all costs and find themselves agreeing to whatever terms are presented instead of negotiating for a more favorable contract.

In the book "The 12 Bad Habits That Hold Good People Back," authors James Waldroop and Timothy Butler, both Harvard Ph.D's, write that people who are phobic about the possibility of a confrontation are afraid that circumstances might spiral out of control and they are uncertain how they will end up. They aren't confident in their ability to survive the loss.

To break the pattern, the doctors set two goals: they desensitize their patients to conflict and then work with them to build their skills in handling conflict.

If you are reluctant to negotiate because you fear confrontation and losing control, do what they did. (1) Place yourself in situations in which you practice negotiation so you can become desensitized to conflict. (2) Improve your negotiating skills through practice and study.

Red Flag #9:
Loss of power

To retain enough power to negotiate effectively, you need to:

- Keep your emotions out of the negotiation process. They don't belong anywhere near you at this point. If your feelings sneak into the negotiations, they will complicate the process. You also risk igniting adverse emotions within the buyer, such as distrust, anxiety, skepticism and even anger. While a controlled emotional exchange may clear the air, it can also cloud your vision and cramp your style. Don't go there. Instead, when you feel your emotions kicking in, breathe deeply, excuse yourself for a moment and walk away. Return when your emotions are subdued.

- Always appear to be a reluctant seller. Perhaps one of the worst mistakes in negotiating is to give away your position when you become anxious and appear to want too much of what the other party is offering. A basic rule of thumb is that the person who appears to want the least will get the most. So, don't be too eager to accommodate. Let the buyers work for their perks.

- Be willing to walk. The skilled negotiator possesses "walk away" power. This means you must decide in advance if you are willing to walk away from the negotiation table and risk losing the sale. You see car buyers do this all the time. They act like they're going to leave the showroom in order to pressure the salesperson into meeting their terms. It often works, but generally that's because the salesperson has determined ahead of time what his bargaining boundaries are. When you give your buyers the impression that you will do whatever it takes to close the sale, you put yourself in a very vulnerable position.

CHAPTER 9

Tactical Maneuvers

"The fellow who says he'll meet you
halfway usually thinks he's standing
on the dividing line."

—Orlando A. Battista

A tactic is a specific action that's undertaken to deal with a specific situation and achieve a specific goal. Ideally, a tactic should move the other person from his or her position while allowing you to remain steadfast.

Tactics are the arms and legs of strategy. You devise your strategies, but it takes targeted tactics to implement them and get results. In this chapter, you'll find tactics formulated to help you reach your goal of selling more new homes through negotiation. These same tactics are also used by the buyer on you, so you'll learn some counter tactics as well.

TACTIC: THE WINCE

This is an overreaction to something the
buyer says or does.

Your buyers make a statement, such as, "The builder in another community is selling his home for $25,000 less than you are."

You wince — make a face — and say, "$25,000! Wow! I don't understand their business strategy! I'm curious. Tell me, why do you think they would do that?"

Remain silent to give the buyers time to respond. This puts the burden on them to substantiate such a price difference. You force them to think about why the other property is less expensive. Is it cheaper materials, less desirable location, fewer amenities, smaller home/ home-site or what?

YOUR COUNTER TACTIC TO THE WINCE

- Here's the unspoken rule about first offers: Never accept them. When the seller accepts the first offer from the buyer, the buyer is left thinking that he could have done better or there is something wrong with the home. The seller is left with the gnawing doubt that he could have received more for his home.

- Know your concessions and incentives ahead of time. By prearranging them and knowing in advance how far you are willing to drop, you will still get what you want even if you end up at your ultimate fallback position.
- Silence. As hard as it might be, bite your tongue and stay tight-lipped.

TACTIC: SILENCE

The most powerful tactic of all in a negotiation is the ability to remain quiet.

As author and motivational speaker Brian Tracy emphasizes, "The only pressure you are allowed to use in a sales presentation is the pressure of silence after you have asked a closing question."

YOUR COUNTER TACTIC TO SILENCE

- More silence. Wait them out.

"Whenever you ask a closing question, shut up. The first person who speaks, loses."

—J. Douglas Edwards

TACTIC: OUTRAGEOUS BEHAVIOR

Beware. The buyer may use fear as a tactic.

Because of the emotions involved in buying a new home, some buyers (and, sadly, even salespeople) practice outrageous behavior by acting erratically, raising their voices or getting too emotionally invested, which creates an impasse.

YOUR COUNTER TACTIC TO OUTRAGEOUS BEHAVIOR

- Time out. Sidestep outrageous behavior by taking a break and allowing for a cool down.
- Set aside tactic. "This is obviously a sensitive issue. Why don't we set this aside, discuss the other issues, and return to this point later?"
- Feel, felt, found: "I understand how you feel. Others have felt the same way, but after thinking about it, here is what they found."

TACTIC: GOOD GUY, BAD GUY

Watch for this team tactic featuring a friend
and an adversary.

You've seen this tactic on police dramas during interrogation scenes. The Bad Guy purposely heightens the tension with outrageous behavior so that the Good Guy can be a calming influence that wins the trust and woos them into believing he is on their side.

In new home sales, it works this way: A buyer's agent tells you, "I'm on your side" or "I am working with you to close this contract." Suddenly, you have someone negotiating for you who isn't really on your side at all. Another approach is for a couple to try the good-guy-bad-guy approach with you in which one of them seems agreeable to everything you say while the other one is argumentative.

When this happens, remember you alone are in control of the negotiation. It is not a team sport.

YOUR COUNTER TACTIC TO GOOD GUY, BAD GUY

- Ask, "You're NOT going to play Good Guy/Bad Guy with me, are you?"

- Ask, "Can you do this without (Bad/Good Guy)?" If they answer "no," then take a timeout until the person in authority is available.

- Dismiss the Good Guy and only deal with the Bad Guy, who is probably the person who is in authority.

TACTIC: RED HERRING

This is a false trail leading away from the true issue.

The Red Herring derives its name from the sport of fox hunting. Hunters competing unfairly would drag a dead fish across the path of the fox after their dogs had passed, diverting the competitor's dogs down a false trail.

Some Potential Buyers try to lead you away from the main issue by making a big deal out of insignificant issues.

To get buyers to refocus on purchasing their new home and less on incidentals, use the foot-in-the-door technique. A study conducted with homeowners in 1996 illustrated that people have a tendency to comply with a major request once they have agreed to a minor one.

Homeowners in an established neighborhood were asked if a large "Drive Carefully" sign could be placed in their front yards. Only 17 percent agreed to allow it. When all the homeowners were asked about putting a three-inch "Be a Safe Driver" sign in their front windows, nearly everyone agreed to do it. Several weeks later, when this same group was asked if the large sign could be placed in their yards, 76 percent said yes.

By getting agreement on smaller items, you have initiated a pattern of positive response and developed a more receptive audience when it's time for the bigger decision.

YOUR COUNTER TACTIC TO
THE RED HERRING

- Employ the set aside tactic. Say to the buyer, "This seems to be a major issue. Why don't we set this aside and establish agreement on the minor issues, then come back to this later?"

- If there is hesitancy by the buyer to set the issue aside ask, "Is this issue your only concern? No? Well, since there are other issues, I promise we will reach a mutually-beneficial resolution on this one later, after we settle a few of the minor issues."

TACTIC: LIMITED AUTHORITY

A final agreement cannot be reached without third-party approval.

In order to come to mutually-agreeable terms and conclude the negotiation process, both sides need to have decision-making power. Limited authority can be used as a delay tactic, but it can only be used twice in the negotiation process. The first time is in the beginning, when Potential Buyers reveal that they are in an information-gathering stage and do not have the complete authority to make the final decision. The second time is at the end.

YOUR COUNTER TACTIC TO
LIMITED AUTHORITY

Limited Authority is more often used at the end of the negotiations. You have given the price or terms and it seems an agreement has been reached, but then the buyer says, "I need to run this by my boss, wife, attorney, banker, other investors, etc."

Your response should be to:

- Reschedule until all parties are available.

- Gain verbal commitment. "I understand, but you will recommend that they accept, won't you?" or "You can't make this kind of decision alone?" With Limited Authority as the negotiating tactic, the buyer will take your offer to the "nonexistent" absentee party and play Good Guy/Bad Guy with you. He'll return and say, "I'm so embarrassed. I felt certain they would go along and, if it were up to me, I would accept; but this is all they would agree to." He remains silent, waiting for a concession from you.

- Withdraw the offer. "Don't be embarrassed. I'm actually relieved. After consideration, I've discovered it would not be advantageous for me to honor the original agreement anyhow." Expect the buyer to then defend his original agreement and you can be the reluctant seller.

TACTIC: FUNNY MONEY

Stretch the price over an extended period of time to make the payment appear nominal and ridiculous.

The buyer says, "I don't know about this. We only wanted to pay $1,500 a month for our mortgage and, with this house, we'll be paying $100 a month more."

You respond by breaking it down to a daily amount. "The difference is only a little more than $3 a day — the price of a cup of coffee. You're not going to let $3 a day stand between you and what you really want and deserve, are you?"

YOUR COUNTER TACTIC TO FUNNY MONEY

- Multiply the aggregate over the period of time, such as a 30- or 15-year mortgage. Suddenly, the difference in the monthly payment doesn't seem as much.

TACTIC: THE VISE

They clamp you in a seemingly immovable position.

The Vise involves backing you into a corner to force you to concede on an issue. Whenever a negotiator employees this tactic, it can be identified by one of these three comments:

1. "You'll have to do better than that."
2. "Let's split the difference."
3. "This is a limited offer."

"You'll have to do better than that."

A general negotiation rule says that whoever states his or her position first usually loses. Rather than saying what she is willing to pay, the Potential Buyer will get you to make a concession first to see how far you are willing to go. Then she will respond with the wince, which will likely lead to another concession. Your Counter Tactic: Respond, "How much better would that have to be?" You get her to state her position first and then you wince.

"Let's split the difference."

When you are asked to split the difference, assume that, if you have the buyer to the point where he is willing to split the difference, he will go further. Your Counter Tactic: "What a shame, and after we've come this far."

Employ the walk away and revert to higher authority, which will allow you to reinitiate a new negotiation with the Good Guy/Bad Guy tactic.

"This is a limited offer."

The buyer has countered with an offer and is creating urgency by emphasizing that the offer won't stay on the table indefinitely. That might be true, but usually it's a ploy to push you to concede to the lesser offer. Your Counter Tactic: Don't be bluffed or pressured and never negotiate in haste. Successful negotiators realize there are few concrete deadlines. Say, "If I have to make a decision now, then my answer is no. However, if you can give me a bit more time, my answer may be yes!"

TACTIC: THE TRIAL BALLOON
Buyers present a hypothetical situation or solution to a challenge.

With this tactic, the buyer voices a hypothetical situation to see if she can get you to change your position. These are teasers to trick you into countering with a better deal for the buyer. The following statements precede Trial Balloons:

- "Just suppose..."
- "I'm not certain..."

- "I may be talking out of school, but..."
- "I probably shouldn't mention this, but what if I could..."

YOUR COUNTER TACTIC TO THE TRIAL BALLOON

- Stand firm. When the buyer floats a Trial Balloon, she has not reached her final position yet. If she is ready to discuss concrete terms, then you can continue with the negotiation.

TACTIC: NIBBLING

They want to make additions to the agreement at the conclusion of the deal.

Once the principal agreement is almost complete, buyers toss out a seemingly spur-of-the-moment, casual request: "Oh, by the way..." or "This will include _____, won't it?"

This really isn't a spur-of-the-moment thought. They've been planning it. And it really isn't casual. It's calculated.

Buyers assume that you will be motivated by a fear of losing the sale after coming this far and having invested so much time. They believe you are now most vulnerable and may be willing to offer additional concessions to keep the deal from falling apart.

"Nibbles" are not deal-breakers so don't fall for this tactic — unless you have anticipated the contract-signing nibbling and were already prepared to honor their request. Remember that buyers want to be sure they got the absolutely best deal. It's your responsibility to show them that they got the best value. Don't allow them to nibble away at your terms.

YOUR COUNTER TACTIC TO NIBBLING

- "Listen, I appreciate your efforts to get the best deal you can; but you have successfully negotiated to the bottom line. You are receiving an exceptional value in purchasing this home and there's just no more room to negotiate."
- Implement the Trade Off.

TACTIC: THE TRADE OFF
If I do that for you, what will you do for me?

Negotiation is a two-way process in which both parties are trying to agree on terms that allow them to get what they want. They are going to pummel you for one exception after another. When you agree to one concession, they will throw another request on the table to see if they can keep you inching toward their desired outcome.

YOUR COUNTER TACTIC TO
THE TRADE OFF

- Any time you make a concession, ask for one in return. This minimizes the value of the concession and will throw a wrench into the grinding-away process. Buyers will eventually realize that, if they keep asking you for concessions, you will respond by asking them for some in return.

TACTIC: GET IT IN WRITING

Think it and ink it. Negotiate on paper.

Put all benefits, warranties, concessions and assurances in writing. People believe the written word, which they can see, over the spoken word, which they can quickly forget. Documenting it also acts as the perfect prompt when selective recall occurs. There is proven power in the written word.

YOUR COUNTER TACTIC TO
GET IT IN WRITING

- When buyers mention a concession you haven't agreed to, tell them, "I don't recall discussing that and we didn't put it in writing anywhere, so I'm not sure where that information is coming from. Can you please enlighten me?"

7 Steps to Move Past an Impasse

Even with the best planning and intentions, you and your Potential Buyers may find yourselves deadlocked because of a disagreement. You just can't seem to get past the impasse. By the way, the word "impasse" is French and literally means a road having no exit; a cul-de-sac. Find yourself in one of those and you'll go in circles until you return to the entrance and use that as an exit point. Same principle applies in negotiating.

You are on the road to successfully concluding the contract when suddenly you and your buyers are going round and round over an issue. When that happens, break the impasse by returning to the beginning.

1. Review the terms you've agreed on previously or that you can easily see eye-to-eye on. This builds a "yes" momentum.

2. Return to prior agreements. "Look, we agreed on this and this and this." or "We've come so far. We're not going to let this stand between us now, are we?"

3. Take a hypothetical approach and issue a Trial Balloon that causes your buyer to look at things under a new light. "We've been talking about a term of 24 months. Just suppose I could extend the terms to 48 months?"

4. Point out the negative consequences of not reaching the agreement, such as someone else may be

considering the same home. Or your company allows cross-selling and you have seven other team members who have access to sell within your neighborhood. It's highly probable that the home your Potential Buyers want could be sold by one of your team members.

5. Appeal to emotions: "I really feel bad. We've had such a great relationship. I don't want this to come between us." Then follow up with silence.

6. Call a time out and take a break so you can clear your head.

7. Use the set-aside tactic and suggest you revisit the issue later.

CHAPTER 10

Can You Hear Me Now?
How to be a Good Listener

"Wisdom is the reward you get
for a lifetime of listening when
you'd have preferred to talk."

—Doug Larson

It's a fact — you gain more knowledge by listening and observing than you do by talking. When you know the right questions to ask, you can sit back and let your buyers provide you with all the information you need in order to negotiate the agreement that will be best for everyone. Active listening also demonstrates that you really are interested in their thoughts, ideas and feelings.

The best way to start discussion when negotiating is with an interview-type question, such as: "Ideally, if you could plot the final outcome of this situation, what would it be?"

Make notes of their responses. You might need to refer to them later.

Tips for listening

- Hear everything your buyers have to say and keep an open mind. Even if their comments in the beginning seem unreasonable, don't respond with a knee-jerk reaction. What you heard might appear inappropriate and you are tempted to jump in and clarify, but hold tight. Hear them out. By the time the buyer finishes the sentence, paragraph or presentation, their points may be both appropriate and acceptable.

- Stay alert and focused. God gave you two ears, two eyes and one mouth, so use them proportionately. Concentrate on your buyers. Pay attention to their body language. Don't interrupt. Question skillfully. Listen attentively. If you allow others the luxury of talking long enough, they will tell you what you need to know.

- Listen for facts versus feelings. Facts cannot be changed. Feelings are perceptions and may easily change or be altered. Be aware of the difference.

- Respond to questions with interest. Seek clarification. Ask, "Why do you feel that way?" or "What do you mean?" Remember that you want to keep this Potential Buyer talking — and revealing.

- Eliminate distractions. Allow no interruptions such as phone calls and visitors. Turn off your cell phone's ringer and let your buyers know you are doing that because you respect their time and don't want to waste it with needless interruptions (the inference here being that they should do the same). Keep your door closed as a signal to others that you don't want to be interrupted. This also cuts down on any disturbances that may occur outside your office.

> "There is no such thing as
> a worthless conversation, provided
> you know what to listen for.
> And questions are the breath
> of life for a conversation."
>
> —James Nathan Miller

Conversational Hints

Words provide clues to what your buyer is thinking or feeling. Listen for these types of words and phrases when negotiating:

- The Legitimizers: Honestly, frankly...
- The Erasers: But, however...
- The Justifiers: I'll try, wish, maybe...
- The Deceptions: I'm no expert...I'm just a country boy...In my humble opinion...
- The Throwaway Before a Major Announcement: By the way. As you are aware....

CHAPTER 11

Learn to Speak Body Language

"The most important thing in
communication is hearing what
isn't said."

—Peter F. Drucker

Psychologists tell us that the spoken word hides more that it reveals. Words come from the intellect and are, therefore, chosen and censored. Nonverbal cues come from the emotional side of the brain and can more easily bypass our subconscious mind.

"Lie to Me" is a popular TV drama that debuted in 2009. It was inspired by the scientific discoveries of a real-life psychologist who reads clues embedded in the human face, body, and voice to expose the truth in criminal investigations. He can tell from the shrug of a shoulder, the movement of a hand, the subtle rise of a lower lip or eyebrow and other nonverbal clues if a criminal is lying.

While you probably won't be able to evaluate people to the same degree as a trained psychologist, you can save time and energy in the negotiating process by paying attention to facial expressions, body posture, subconscious gestures and eye movements. Since visible nonverbal behavior serves as an informal lie detector, you should, whenever possible, avoid negotiating by phone.

Your nonverbal communication should always reinforce the fact that you are both interested and invested in your buyers and in their well-being.

How do nonverbal communication cues affect conversation?

Anytime you interact with Potential Buyers, you and they are giving and receiving countless clues about what each of you is thinking and feeling. Observe the way your buyers listen, talk, move and react.

Invade their personal space and do you pick up on subliminal messages they're sending of intimacy, dominance, connection or aggression? Does your body language match your words, reinforcing that your buyers can trust you?

Pay close attention when your Potential Buyers speak. Is the sound of their voice broadcasting confidence, sarcasm, timidness, anger, distraction, annoyance, warmth, eagerness, doubt? Note its inflection, tone, pace, intensity, fluctuation and volume.

Listen With Your Eyes.

According to psychologists, nonverbal communication can affect the spoken word in five ways that are easy to spot.

Gestures can:

1. Contradict our words. Example: A Potential Buyer says he totally agrees with you, but tightens his mouth to avoid saying what he truly feels.
2. Complement what we're saying. Example: An impasse has been avoided, the buyers are pleased, say "great job" and give you a reassuring pat on the back.
3. Reinforce a comment. Example: The buyer says he agrees with you and nods his head.
4. Substitute for speaking. Example: She doesn't like the compromise solution you've offered and rolls her eyes, but doesn't say anything.
5. Emphasize something being said. Example: The Potential Buyer pounds the table while making a point.

Observe their faces, eyes, hands and posture.

Face

A face is a blank canvas that displays the obvious and most expressive manifestations of a person's feelings. Facial expressions are universal and reveal the emotions behind the spoken words. They provide us with intimate and immediate feedback on what is being spoken. For example:

- Rubbing eyes or ears with hand may indicate doubt or lack of interest.

- Stroking the chin shows thoughtfulness or consideration.

- Pinching the bridge of the nose demonstrates either great concern or a splitting headache.

- Leaning back and supporting the head with both hands translates into an air of superiority, authority or being at ease.

- Rubbing the nape of neck signifies frustration or tension.

- Hand to mouth reflects shock, astonishment or an attempt to avoid saying something.

- Tugging at the ear may mean the buyer wants to interrupt.

- Placing chin in hand and lowering the eyes is a sure sign of boredom.

Hands and Arms

While watching the face for nonverbal communication, don't ignore your buyers' hands and arms. They can provide you with even more insight into their mindset. Think about the instant impression you get from a firm handshake, a restraining grip on your arm, an embracing hug, or a weak tap on your shoulder.

More cues and clues:

- Strumming fingers signify impatience.
- Clenched hands represent strong disagreement.
- Two hands clenched together show that your client is feeling intimidated and suspicious.
- Wringing hands can mean extreme anxiety.
- Gently rubbing one palm with the other hand shows expectation and delight.
- Joining hands in upward prayer-like manner (steepling) indicates self-confidence and superiority.
- Hands joined behind the back while standing reflects superiority or supervisory attitude.
- Crossed arms reflect a need for protection or self-defensiveness. This is the most important position for a sales professional to recognize because your client is demonstrating that he does not want to be involved with you or your proposal, or she does not believe you.

Posture

Posture is as much about a person's psyche and attitude as it is about the physical structure of the skeletal support system. Take the time to study your buyer's posture and read the messages it's sending.

- Leaning forward indicates the buyers are interested. You have their full attention and they could be ready for the close.

- Leaning back is a sign that they feel threatened. Your buyers are not yet ready to close, so they're widening the space between you. You must bring them back toward you.

- Removing and cleaning glasses is an attempt to gain time, stall or think about something else.

- Putting the glasses' earpiece in mouth shows that your buyer is trying to keep from speaking.

- Eyes up while speaking can mean several things. After asking a question, if their eyes go up, they are carefully considering the reply. If they are asking the question and their eyes go up, they are carefully considering what they are saying.

- Eyes and head go down. If you ask a person a question and the eyes and head shift downward at the same time, you have a lie.

Nonverbal communication should reinforce what your Potential Buyers are saying. If you notice inconsistencies, follow up by asking questions.

CHAPTER 12

Closing the Gap

"In business, you don't get what you
deserve. You get what you negotiate."

—Chester L. Karrass

The goal of negotiation is to navigate Potential Buyers through the decision-making process and lead them to a point where they feel comfortable agreeing to the terms you propose. This getting-to-yes process can take different routes, so be prepared to be diverted.

Detours are usually the result of some obstacle that has blocked the chosen pathway. In driving, these obstacles could be road construction, accidents, storm damage, disabled vehicles or debris. In negotiations for a new home, these obstacles come in the form of objections from the buyers.

Someone once told me; "Obstacles are those frightful things you see when you take your eyes off your goal."

To keep your eyes on the goal and on the bottom line, here are appropriate responses to some common obstacles your buyers will throw at you.

Obstacle Objection #1:

"I don't want to go through the trouble of signing a contract yet. Just tell the builder I'm making this offer."

Before you even begin the process of negotiating for a new home, establish if your buyer sincerely wants to own one. If there is no desire, there is nothing to negotiate.

When a person is committed to purchasing a home, validate that desire by getting him to hand you a deposit. The purchase of a new home is personal and you can't get much more personal than being handed someone's money and signature.

While the goal is always to capture those signatures, there are buyers who are stubborn and will ask you to first present a verbal offer to the builder without a check and a contract. When this happens, stand firm in your position to only present a contract and a check to the builder.

> Potential Buyer: "Rather than prepare the paper-work, can you first check with your builder and see if this is even possible?"

> YOU: "For any type of offer to be valid, considera-tion and an agreement are necessary. In other words, to have a valid and binding agreement, we need to prepare the paperwork, complete with your request and the initial investment. Otherwise, your

offer won't be considered. So, let's take care of the paperwork so that I can present your offer today to the builder along with your deposit check, okay?"

Potential Buyer: "We would be much more comfortable if you would simply run this by the builder first verbally and see where he stands. If it's acceptable, we can prepare the paperwork afterward."

YOU: "In addition to not having a valid agreement, Mr. and Mrs. Potential Buyer, without the paperwork and the deposit check, my builder would not even review your request; and without him looking at it, your answer is an automatic 'no.' However, if I present your request with consideration and an agreement, then possibly the answer would be 'yes' or he'd at least give us a counteroffer. So, as you see, in order to move your request forward, we must prepare the paperwork first. Let's do that now, so I can present your request by the end of the business day."

This approach has the added benefit of uncovering how serious your buyers really are. If they continue to hedge about taking this step, they might not be earnest enough to engage in a negotiation.

Obstacle Objection #2:

"I Want To Think About It"

"I want to think about it" or "I want to think it over" is the most common objection you will come across. In the best of situations and under the most ideal conditions, you will hear this almost every time you try to close a sale. The problem with "I want to think about it" is that it's a broad statement that is not narrowed to any one specific concern. Buyers usually won't tell you why they want to think about it or disclose the reasons for their reluctance. This leaves you in limbo.

Potential Buyer: "I need to think it over."

YOU: "Hey, I don't blame you. I would want to think about it, too. Buying a brand new home is a big decision, isn't it?"

Potential Buyer: "It sure is and it isn't one I want to make quickly."

YOU: "I completely understand that! What might be helpful is if I assemble some relevant information for you to take home that will assist in your decision-making process. Would that be okay with you?"

Potential Buyer: "Yes."

YOU: "Good. Now, to make sure that I include information that relates to where you are in making a decision to buy a new home, I'd like to ask you just a couple of questions. Okay?"

Potential Buyer: "Sure."

In a very casual, conversational manner, ask these questions as you assemble the information packet.

YOU: "First, you mentioned you love this area. Is that correct?"

Potential Buyer: "Yes, I love the area."

YOU: "Your impression of the community is favorable, right?"

Potential Buyer: "Oh yeah! The community is wonderful!"

YOU: "Now, what about the home? How do you feel about the one you have selected?"

Potential Buyer: "We really like it."

YOU: "So, what is holding you back from making this home yours? You like the community, the homes and the area, but you're still hesitant to move forward. Do you mind my asking if it's the price of the home or the financial arrangements?"

If you have come this far and your Potential Buyers are genuinely interested, then most likely their reluctance to commit is rooted in a money issue. It might be the price of the home. It could be that they need to sit down with a lender because they don't know if they will qualify to buy. Or perhaps they think they can snap up a better deal elsewhere.

If the buyers are reluctant to move ahead, ask yourself:

- If you give them more time to decide — if they wait another week or so — what will change?
- What's going to be different later that will help them make the decision to buy a new home in my community?

I'll tell you one thing that will change for certain. The sales cycle will be broken. You will be history — and here's why. People are emotional beings. Each choice we make is flushed through channels of emotions before it ever gets caught in the mainstream of logic.

Instead of letting a Potential Buyer walk away from a negotiation, make every effort to determine the root of their hesitation. Then address it immediately. Don't get desperate and start throwing concessions at them, but zoom in and provide the answers they need to move on to "yes!"

Obstacle Objection #3:

"I want another opinion."

The second most common objection is one in which Potential Buyers say they can't close because they must check with a third party, such as a spouse, lawyer, CPA, business partner or investor.

> Potential Buyer: "This seems to be perfect, but before making my final decision, I need to run this by my banker."

> YOU: "I understand. Then am I correct in assuming that you are totally satisfied and there is no question in your mind that owning this magnificent home is the right thing for you to do?"

> Potential Buyer: "Yes, I'm certain. I just want my banker to look it over."

> YOU: "Great! Then the only question is whether your banker says it's the right thing to do. Is that correct?"

> Potential Buyer: "That's it."

> YOU: "Mr. and Mrs. Potential Buyer, may I ask you a question? (pause) Just suppose your banker was present at this very moment and she advised you to take advantage of this gorgeous home. Would you act today?"

> Potential Buyer: "I suppose we would."

> YOU: "Unfortunately, she is not with us today. However, prior to your speaking with her and to

guarantee that someone else will not purchase your home, let's prepare the paperwork now and we will make the sale 'subject to' your banker's approval. This way the process has begun, we've secured your homesite and if, by chance, she doesn't agree, we will simply start over. That makes sense, doesn't it?"

Obstacle Objection #4:

"This house costs too much."

Does it really? Maybe not. Maybe your buyers are comparing it to a competitor's home that's been discounted. Or maybe the amount exceeds what your buyers have budgeted.

There is a world of difference between your Potential Buyers' willingness to pay and their ability to pay. To identify where the problem lies and why they think the cost is too high, you need to readjust their perception about this objection. Realign their focus off the total selling price of the home and on to something more productive by showing them how to calculate the cost difference per day.

For example, suppose the competition is discounting homes by $20,000 and your buyer asks you to do the same thing. How would you respond?

> YOU: "Let's review the $20,000 amount that you are asking the builder to reduce from the price. I sincerely understand where you're coming from and appreciate your concern for wanting to remain within budget. I know $20,000 seems like a major amount, but let's break it down."

Hand the Potential Buyers a calculator and allow them to work through the math with you.

> YOU: At today's interest rates, for every $1,000 you finance, your monthly investment is $7. (The number will change according to prevailing rates, of

course, but the method remains the same.) That means the $20,000 difference you seek is, in reality, $140 a month. Now, I realize that, at first glance, $140 per month seems like a lot; but let's break that amount down on a daily basis. In a 30-day month, the $140 becomes only $4.67 a day. Mr. and Mrs. Potential Buyer, I bet you spend $4.67 a day on bottled water, a white mocha latte, a magazine or other inconsequential items, don't you? Well, for the cost of even one of these, you can own the brand new home of your dreams.

"I know this may seem ridiculous, but if you reflect on it, $20,000 isn't really that much over the long term. So, we'll present your offer, but if it isn't accepted by the builder, are you going to allow $4.67 a day stand in the way of owning the home you really want and deserve?"

Obstacle Objection #5:

"I just can't decide."

You've delivered a brilliant presentation and effectively tapped into their desires to own a new home, but your Potential Buyers are increasingly hesitant and indecisive. Rather than to continue speaking in terms of the Potential Buyers' gain, shift gears and talk about what they will lose by not taking action.

> YOU: "Mr. and Mrs. Potential Buyer, I can see you really love this home. Am I right?"

> Potential Buyer: "Yes, that's right."

> YOU: "I also sense you are hesitant to make a commitment and you're having a hard time making up your mind. So, let me offer this suggestion. Since this is a popular community and this is the only home currently at this location/price/under these terms, it's likely that another buyer will come along and purchase your home before you do.

Should this happen, let's have a Plan B in place. Why don't we select a backup home that is almost as desirable as your first choice?"

> Now — and this is critical — remain perfectly silent!

> Potential Buyer: "We don't want a home that's almost as desirable. We want this one."

> YOU: "I certainly understand that. Then shall we move forward and make this one yours? The initial

investment is only $____. I'm assuming you will be using a personal check for the deposit, right?"

This strategy may not work 100 percent of the time. For instance, the Potential Buyer may respond with, "We'll take our chances" ... or ... "If it's meant to be, it's meant to be."

> YOU: "Well, that sounds very accommodating, but there is also something to be said for going for what you want in life. Are you sure that, if someone were to take your home, it would be okay with you and you would be willing to settle for something you might find less desirable ... something that falls a little short of being your ideal dream home?"

The Potential Buyer may now respond with, "That is really pushy" or "We are just not comfortable going any further."

> YOU: "I understand. It's just that, in the past, several couples just like you have come back after a few days only to discover their homes were owned by someone else. I don't want that to happen to you. You know what I'm saying?"

Obstacle Objection #6:

"Looks like we're in a Catch-22 situation."

Sometimes, to get closure, you have to offer a take-it-or-leave-it solution and lay your cards on the table.

> YOU: "The reality is, Mr. Potential Buyer, that this home will sell — and it will sell at this price and under these terms and conditions. So, what you need to decide is if you will be the one to buy it or not. Unfortunately, it seems that we're in a Catch-22 situation. We can't move forward under the terms you are seeking because they don't reflect the true value of this home, and you don't want to buy it at the price set forth by the builder."

Pause for a moment and then continue.

"Look, I'm a realist and I do want you to be comfortable with your new home purchase. In fact, I pride myself on not submitting the paperwork on a new home until the buyer is more excited about it than I am. Obviously, you aren't. So, the bottom line is that, if you're looking for discounts and concessions instead of a quality lifestyle and stable home values, then this community isn't right for you.

I know that you want the best price available and I respect that. By the same token, I hope you can appreciate that this isn't only the <u>best price</u> I can offer you, but it's also the absolute lowest, take-it-or-leave-it price I can offer you."

Another approach:

> YOU: Mr. and Mrs. Potential Buyer, I'll admit that not everyone can afford our new homes. That is a reality I have to face and, if you're in that position, then please let me know and I'll show you homes that are in your price range. However, if the sales price fits within your budget, then let's talk about value. Let's review what you'll be getting when you buy one of these new homes in this lovely community."

From this point, you sell features and benefits, such as the home's curb appeal, lot size, architectural style, infrastructure (water, sewer, sidewalks, tree-lined streets), community amenities, location, number of bedrooms, construction quality, builder's reputation and awards, appliances, "green" features, school district desirability, neighborhood conveniences and proximity to water/mountains/beach/city/country/recreation.

This is a take-it-or-leave-it close and it signals the end of negotiations. The reality is that your buyers will never tire of receiving concessions. They will always want more — a lower price, an upgrade at no charge, paid closing costs, etc. — but you have to set limits and stick to them. In many cases, the buyer just wants to be sure that you have presented the best terms possible and that they are leaving nothing on the table because they stopped negotiating too soon. With the take-it-or-leave-it close, you send that message loud and clear.

CHAPTER 13

Show Me The Money!

"Knowing the 'counters' to every
strategy is as important as knowing
the strategy itself."

—Dr. Jim Hennig

I've said it before, but it bears repeating: Your strategy begins by gaining the Potential Buyer's commitment that he really wants to own a home or homesite.

Potential Buyer: "We want to make an offer." or "What's the bottom line?" or "Do you think they will take less?" or "What's the best you'll do?"

YOU: "That question sounds like you're interested in owning this home. Is that right?" or "Am I hearing you correctly, that you're ready to become the owner of this home today?"

If the Potential Buyer responds "no" to your question, there is no reason to continue discussing price. Instead, wince and say:

YOU: "Really! Why not?"

Do not continue the negotiating process without your Potential Buyer's confirmation that he sincerely wants to be a homeowner. Stand firm. Remember that the negotiation process is fueled by the buyer's desire to own.

Once you have firmly secured the commitment, you will face additional obstacles — all related in some form or another — to the price of the home. In addition to the responses mentioned in the previous chapter, here are specific ones to price objections.

Obstacle Objection #7:

"Will You Take Less Than the Listed Price?"

Potential Buyer: "We would like to make an offer." or "Will you take less than the listed price?" or "What's the best you can do?" or "What's the bottom line?"

Response #1

> YOU: "That question sounds like you're interested in owning this home. Is that right?" Or "Am I understanding you correctly? You're ready to become the owner of this home today?"
>
> Potential Buyer: "Yes, but only if we can get it at the right price (or at a deal)."
>
> YOU: "Of course. So let's be clear about what you mean when you say 'the right price.' Mr. Potential Buyer, with today's technology, nearly everyone has access to a computer. In fact, the vast majority of new home buyers begin their search online. With all this information available at our fingertips, it isn't surprising that anyone can go online and find out how much you paid for your home. So, let me ask you something. How would you feel if you paid several thousand dollars more for your home than your neighbor … and he knew it? The reality is that, if we indiscriminately offered different discounts to different buyers, everyone could know what everyone paid. This knowledge could not only breed resentment, but would also affect property values.

Mr. and Mrs. Potential Buyer, are you familiar with how true real estate value is determined? In reality, the developer/builder or the salesperson representing the home/homesite does not determine value. Value is based on comparable sales. In other words, a professional appraiser says the property's market value is a certain amount based on recent sales of comparable properties.

If someone purchased a comparable home yesterday for $350,000 and today you bought the same model for $300,000, and tomorrow someone negotiates the builder down to $275,000, then what is the true value of that home?

Mr. and Mrs. Potential Buyer, we do everything we can to protect the value of homes within our neighborhood and, as a result, the equity in your home. To accomplish that, we must maintain consistent pricing for every buyer. If a brand new home is going to be one of your single largest investments, then isn't it reassuring to know that you are doing business with a builder who is concerned with guarding your personal equity and protecting the assessment value of the community?"

Response #2

YOU: "In many ways, a discount is really an admission of guilt by builders that they made a mistake and overcharged many other home buyers in the past. By lowering the price, now they're saying, 'We overcharged them at first, but this is what the home is really worth.' While this seems great for the buyer, what about the other homeowners?

How would you feel if you paid the full price only to learn that all of your neighbors paid less?

Beyond the builder's admission of guilt, this pricing strategy is the fastest, surest way to insure a meltdown of your personal equity and the meltdown of equity in the entire neighborhood. You won't get that from this builder or this community. That isn't how we do business."

This strategy is equally effective when negotiating with a buyer's agent, presumably someone who truly understands and appreciates the nuances of property values, investment stability and home equity.

Obstacle Objection #8:

"We could have bought months/years ago for a lot less money."

This is a common objection from buyers who are trying to use hindsight as a ploy to negotiate a better price. Your strategy is to help them discover that their failure to act in the past will only cost them more in the future.

> Potential Buyer: "We could have bought the same property for $___ last month/year."
>
> YOU: "You are not going to let that happen again, are you?"

If they say "no," proceed to contracts. If they hesitate, continue talking.

> YOU: "What's important is not to focus on what you could have done in the past, but on what you will do in the future. If it was a mistake not to buy then, how will you feel if you miss the opportunity to buy today and the price goes up in a month/year from now? Let's go ahead and secure your home today and next month/year you can sit back and realize you received today's best value at a time that's perfect for you."

Often, a change of perception is all that's needed to retool a regret into an opportunity.

Obstacle Objection #9:

"The competition will discount their homes. Why won't you?"

The strategy is twofold, so there are two scripts. In the first script, you clarify why they haven't purchased from the builder who is offering generous discounts. Although this is a bold move, if the other house were truly a "deal," they would not be talking to you.

The goal of the second script is to guide them into the realization that someone else's discounted deal may not be to their advantage.

Script 1

Potential Buyer: "Your competition is making better deals" or "will cut their prices" or "is offering substantial incentives."

YOU: "Mr. Potential Buyer, I do not want to appear discourteous, but I'm puzzled. If you feel it's such a great price, why haven't you bought one of their homes?"

Remain silent and let them state their reasons. They may say they like the homes but not the community or location; or they like the price, but not the designs, quality, builder, etc.

YOU: "Mr. Potential Buyer, it seems as though price is not the real issue for you. What you're really concerned with is obtaining the best value. Is that correct? Let's take a moment to discuss what's truly the best value for your family and/or investment needs."

Script 2

Potential Buyer: "I like your home, but the competition is priced $20,000 less." or "The competition is offering to discount their homes by $20,000."

YOU: "I don't understand their business strategy! Mr. and Mrs. Potential Buyer, why do you think they would do that?"

Potential Buyer: "They are having a difficult time selling their homes." or "They need to sell their homes." or "Have you looked outside recently? There's nothing but 'For Sale' signs up and down the street. Property just isn't selling, so I guess they want to do something to attract buyers." or "I don't know why and I don't care. I just know they are."

Here are some ways you can respond to their request for a discount:

YOU: "May I ask a question, please? Is a brand new home one of the single largest investments of your life?"

Potential Buyer: "Of course!"

YOU: "Will you be making one of the largest investments of your life based purely on incentives or how much the home is discounted? Every builder wants to get the maximum selling price for his homes.

Wouldn't you agree? So, are you really getting a discount or are you paying the maximum amount they can get? I ask this because, if you think about it, in reality the discounted price is all the home is really worth.

Are you comfortable with the thought that they are cutting prices and deals? I'm just a little concerned. Will you ever know if you got the best price or did someone else get a better deal than you did? And if they are having a difficult time selling their homes, will you be comfortable making the single largest investment of your life in a community where homes aren't selling? How will this affect their long-term value?

Our builder knows what his homes are worth. He built value into these new homes from their blueprint conception. He has a reputation for not sacrificing value for quick sales. He didn't cut corners or use less expensive materials when he was building the homes so he could afford to reduce prices later when the market tightened. If he didn't discount the homes when they were under construction, why would he discount them now?"

Obstacle Objection #10:

"We can get a better per-square-foot price than this."

Basing the price on a cost-per-square-foot basis is a conventional approach, but a fallible one. You can overcome this obstacle with your buyers when you demonstrate the flaw in their thinking.

> YOU: "We have never looked at it that way because there are so many variables — such as materials, warranties and customer satisfaction — when determining the price of a home. I'm curious. Are you looking for a new home based solely on price per square foot?"

> Potential Buyer: "No, but we do want the best price."

> YOU: "Great! What I'm hearing you say is that you're looking for the best value in a new home. Is that correct?"

> Potential Buyer: What's the difference?

> YOU: "That's a good question. A lot of people don't understand the difference between the price they pay and the value they receive. Basically, the price of a home is, of course, its cost—what you pay for it. The home's value, however, has to do with its worth. For example, if our homes include high-end appliances, better quality construction, eco-friendly features, excellent builder reputation, a desirable

neighborhood, and a beautifully landscaped yard, it would probably be priced more than a similar home in an adjacent neighborhood; but its value would be much greater because, with all the additional benefits, you would be getting more for your money.

Settling on a square-foot price is difficult because a home's true value is not determined by square footage, but by component parts. Let me give you an example. The price of carpet is $___ per square yard, while tile is $___ per square foot. What we need to do is determine what you would like in your home and then we price the home according to the materials we use. That makes sense, doesn't it?

In searching for a new home, there are three points to consider: Less expensive price per square foot, quality and service. Unfortunately, as a builder/developer, we can only deliver two of the three at the same time. Which two are you most interested in receiving?"

Obstacle Objection #11:

"We can buy a bigger/larger home from the competition for the same amount of money."

The Potential Buyer may try to negotiate by stating the competition builds larger homes than yours, but you know they come with fewer custom features.

Response #1

> YOU: "Mr. and Mrs. Potential Buyer, we don't just build what is known as a big-box floor plan with a lot of square footage at the cheapest price. Frankly, that's an approach that lacks quality, innovation and is not in touch with current trends. Our commitment is to design custom features that reflect your personal taste and make your home as unique as your individual signature. We concentrate on craftsmanship, superior materials and a lifelong commitment to customer satisfaction.

All things considered, if price per square foot and a big-box floor plan is what you base your comparisons on, we may not have what you're looking for. Now that you understand our value is in the total package, can we take a few moments to discuss what features are important to you and your family? Once we know what you really need and want, we can calculate a price on a home that you would take pride in owning."

Response #2

> YOU: "Mr. and Mrs. Potential Buyer, the basic big-box floor plan you are considering is already outdated. Ten years from now, when you may want to sell, you will be marketing a 10-year-old home with a 15- or 20-year-old floor plan. Our designs are cutting-edge and current. Because they are kept up to date, they will hold their value for years to come, which is an important factor when it is time to sell.

There are many ways to cut prices when building a home, and buying a big-box floor plan is one of them; but it may not be the best decision for you. Let's discuss and review floor plans that mirror your personal taste and will still retain their value in the future."

A final thought: If your Potential Buyers aren't throwing out any obstacles, then you probably aren't on the path to a sale. Perceive each obstacle as an opportunity to negotiate and navigate your way back.

In Conclusion

"There comes a time when the risk
to remain tight in the bud is
more painful than the risk it takes
to blossom."

—French Proverb

My wife enjoys gardening and all the labor-intensive effort it takes to produce a flower or vegetable. One of the plants she grows is called a moon flower. It has a large, beautiful white flower that opens around dusk. It only blooms during the night so it can be pollinated by moths. By morning, the blossom dies and a new bud appears.

For the moon flower to continue its growth cycle, the old pedals must be discarded daily to make way for the new bloom.

There is a life lesson here. Too often we want to hold on to what isn't working anymore — old sales techniques, outdated beliefs, obsolete systems and strategies. There's comfort in the familiar, so we're reluctant to let them go and move into the unknown.

It's said that a good leader is one who can tell others how to bloom through the cycles and seasons of life; but a great leader is one who can guide others into self-discovery so they can tap into their own potential and drop those passé pedals that continue to cling.

I strive for the "great leader" category, encouraging you to take the risk and blossom instead of remaining "tight in the bud."

As part of that, I wrote this book to shed light on — and shed misconceptions about — the process of negotiation. I truly believe that, if you're willing to give it a go, the knowledge you find within these pages can seed your sales so they flourish under any circumstance.

Although this is the end of the book, it isn't the final chapter. You will write that.

W. Myers Barnes, President
Myers Barnes Associates

Afterword

Isn't It Time?

Come to the edge, he said.

We might fall, the people cried.

Come to the edge!

It's too high!

COME TO THE EDGE!

They came.

He pushed,

And they flew.

I beckon all homebuilding professionals to come to the edge. Stop worrying about discounting, incentives, sales events and competition. Leave all that behind and come to the edge ... to the place where you draw the line and say, "I'll go this far and no further."

I won't continue competing against builders with sharper pencils than mine. I won't keep justifying the prices of my homes instead of selling buyers on their value. I won't keep making excuses for why I'm not turning a profit. I am the producer of my circumstances; not the product of them.

I won't allow others to define my business. I will write that definition myself. It won't be easy, but I will take a stand on the edge ... and I will fly.

Contact the Author

Join the individuals, companies and organizations nationwide that are experiencing dynamic results from following the advice of one of the world's most exciting authors, consultants and motivational speakers. For more published material authored by Myers Barnes or to schedule private consultation or a seminar, contact:

Myers Barnes Associates, Inc.
P.O. Box 50
Kitty Hawk, NC 27949
Phone (252) 261-7611
Fax (252) 261-7615
E-mail: solutions@myersbarnes.com
Web site: www.myersbarnes.com

Follow Myers on Facebook and Twitter. Subscribe to his blog at www.myersbarnes.com/blog.

Other Books by Myers Barnes

Closing Strong - The Super Sales Handbook
How to Close Every Sale

Closing Strong—The Super Sales Handbook presents a powerful, comprehensive collection of proven strategies used by celebrated sales stars including concise real life situations and actual "dialogue" that you can use to gain immediate advantage and close more sales.

Myers shows you how to:

- Contact and qualify prospects
- Obtain new clients
- Use the telephone to build urgency
- Turn objections to your advantage
- Know exactly what to say to win the sale

New Home Sales in a Nutshell
How to Make Every Sale - Now!

New Home Sales in a Nutshell provides invaluable scripts and strategies for success in a challenged market. This powerful manual will help you realize your goals and vastly improve your conversion ratio. Whether you need solid closing strategies or tactics to get buyers' agents to work with you, New Home Sales in a Nutshell will have you closing sales like clockwork.

This step-by-step guide provides:

- Tried and True New Home Sales Tactics
- Scripts for Success in a Challenged Market
- Sensible Solutions & Practical Negotiation Tips
- Bold Responses to Every Possible Buyer Objection
- Ten Closing Strategies that will Double Your Conversions

Reach the Top In New Home & Neighborhood Sales

How to Create Win-Win Situations -
The New Home Sales Bible!

Reach the Top is a goldmine of practical, hands-on information that works every day in real world selling situations. Carry it with you and overcome objections as they happen. Read one short chapter in Reach The Top and watch your sales results improve immediately.

You'll discover:

- How to professionally meet and greet clients
- How to effectively qualify prospects
- How to close with the most powerful techniques available

- How to follow up to convert your prospect to a customer
- How to make customers your partners for life
- How to secure an endless stream of referrals

Hundreds of strategies and sales methods to help you get even the toughest buyer to say "Yes"

Supercharged Sales

Guarantee Your Success

Supercharged Sales means pushing your beliefs and expanding your way of thinking—to be better and smarter than your competition and to achieve far beyond the results you want in your personal and business life. Whether you are at the top of your company or bound and determined to get there, this is the one "cookbook" for success that will earn your seal of approval. Supercharged Sales puts the fun back into your business.

You will learn:

- How your customers want to buy new homes
- Eight techniques that sell the co-broke community on selling with you
- Five common selling errors with real world solutions
- The art of making better decisions
- The titan's secrets to closing the sale

Index

_____

_____

_____

_____

_____

_____

_____

_____

_____

_____

_____

_____

_____

_____

_____

_____